Advance praise for *The Reckless Hope of Scoundrels*

"As one might guess from its title, *The Reckless Hope of Scoundrels*, Tony Burnett's first collection of poems is about frustration as much as about hope, especially in the realms of love and technology, areas in which Burnett seems to feel left behind, like many of us of a certain age. Yet the hope shines through as evidenced by tongue-in-cheek attitudes and wordplay, even when he claims to be 'mud stuck in funk.'" - Scott Wiggerman, author of *Leaf and Beak: Sonnets* and *Presence*

"Climb on board for a kaleidoscopic road trip through the poetic countryside with songwriter and storyteller Tony Burnett. Love is nearby but often elusive, as in one poem's closing lines: 'The gull departs, wings twitching,/ the last vestige of romance/ gripped in its beak.' Along the way, Burnett writes about Mayan temples, raptors, border colonias, fracking for oil, and outdoor work, where this refrain applies also to his writing: 'Let the tool do the work.'" - Chip Dameron, author *of Drinking From the River: New & Selected Poems 1975 - 2015*

"Fearless, irreverent, caroming between the world's end and the most intimate of moments, Tony Burnett's poetry collection, *The Reckless Hope of Scoundrels*, is a rip-roaring rodeo ride through a world tilting on its axis. This collection is filled with insightful music, both gentle and blunt. The book creates a space where '[l]iar's words stink, mullet bloated and bursting/near brackish backwater on a red tide bay....' Burnett has an ear for the subtle notes that string each disparate piece together in a necklace of smooth sound. This collection, spanning three decades, is carved from Texas' mesquite and bursts from the Lone Star's thick clay with a secular, singing magic. - Joani Reese-- author of *Final Notes, Dead Letters*, and her nearest, a hybrid collection of poetry and flash fiction, *Night Chorus*, from the LitFest Press

The

RECKLESS

HOPE of

SCOUNDRELS

The

RECKLESS

HOPE   *of*

SCOUNDRELS

selected poems 1985 -2015

Tony

Burnett

copyright 2016 by Tony Burnett

published by Kallisto Gaia Press

Davilla TX 76523

www.kallistogaiapress.org

Library of Congress Publication-in-data are

available from the Library of Congress

ISBN-13: 978-0692667255 (Kallisto Gaia Press)

ISBN-10: 0692667253

DEDICATION

For Judy K. LeBlanc (1956 - 1971)

"I long ago abandoned the notion of a life without storms, or a world without dry and killing seasons.

— Kay Redfield Jamison

TABLE OF CONTENTS

Broken Windows

Stained Glass

Broken Mirrors

Shards

Acknowledgements

BROKEN

WINDOWS

FIRST SEASON

I asked Spring to spare a kiss

and found it laced with laudanum.

Bound by Muscadine and tendrils

of Morning Glory, I awakened.

Sun-steamed fibrillae of desire

dancing on my loins, a longing;

usher me into your rapture,

enclose me in your petals.

May, your foliage captures me

and steals last Winter's mettle.

Cooled by breeze on morning mist

skin fire blazing settles.

Released from bonds of April's arms

a swim in glacial rivers

within a breath of picnic held

on mattresses of meadow grasses.

Dare I risk another kiss?

I could not bear to forget this.

MERMAID

From the sand, the gilded orb

dangling over the horizon

silhouettes your torso.

The waves, almost dormant now,

ripple through your fingers.

      if only -

Fingers rise in unison,

a contrapuntal fugue conducted

from the terminus of outstretched arms

droplets falling cast

prismatic hue against the grey.

      if only -

In grey pirouette, longing more for moon

than shore,

your attention disposes of me

clumped on the sand,

yearning.

      if only -

If only I were light.

If only in another time.

If only I could swim to you.

LOVE SONG OF THE LAUGHING GULL

A laughing gull thrusts our passion into this technocracy

where love songs are limited to 140 characters.

There are no damsels in distress.

No Daughters of Aphrodite guard their maidenheads

with grace and manual dexterity

waiting to be plied with mead.

Click on the photo to view my profile.

Fill out this questionnaire.

Wait for the background check

while the gull giggles

and ingests another morsel of time.

Intimacy is exchanging recipes

in the produce department

Fondle a melon if you dare

or a dark knobby cucumber.

The gull departs, wings twitching,

the last vestige of romance

gripped in its beak.

LOVE NOTE ON PAPER #1

INFATUATION

I am not acknowledged by technology,

a super saver with paper coupons.

Debit or credit? How about a check?

Check your bags?

I have accumulated too much baggage for a baggage check.

a story too long for a tweet,

a tale too twisted for a text.

AND YET,

here we are,

arms and eyes open,

mouths

about to spout the sport

of intoxicated infatuation.

LOVE NOTE ON PAPER #2

TRAINING

I have become intoxicated from sharing your breath.

As if bitten, your lips recoil from mine.

Your eyelids flip open like cartoon window shades

 The constellations in your eyes shift a dimension.

Are you okay? I ask.

Why are you being so weird? Your eyes were open!

Yes, I admit. *So?*

You're supposed to close your eyes when kissing, you insist.

But how would I see the down of your lashes against your cheek

   or your elegant fingertips break the promise of my skin?

Let's try this again, you say.

   Keep your eyes closed.

   We have to get this right.

LOVE NOTE ON PAPER #3

TEASING

like time on a carnival ride,

the swirling love loop moment halts,

a monument, as love quick beats the heart.

A flash of time for hand held baskets

and summer picnic pastorals.

Riff on sexual desires and future progeny,

a boy, a girl or two to lengthen the moment.

Seconds become minutes on the geographical clock

as we piss away the generations. Taught to live

by the wise elders.

A string theory of blissful continuity

broken only by

the inevitable deterioration

 of communication,

Another extinction.

THE RECKLESS HOPE OF SCOUNDRELS

1.

Yesterday's babies crave the gray dust of Apocalypse.

Voluptuous vixens wailing death metal harmonies,

their funhouse painted fingers beat erasers

against titanium slates,

echoing heartbeats of old souls and reckless victims.

All knowing.

All gray.

Irreverent reboot.

Sweet minimalist joy of building from scratch - no instructions.

New construction on foundations of skeletons ground to dust;

mixed with spittle, blood and kiln-fired hope.

See the future rolling across the prairie, an F-5 tornado;

wet, black and six miles wide.

Raise those middle fingers one last time

and laugh.

2.

In yesterday's dream I was a Freedom Fighter,

a terrorist with a well-funded PR firm.

Globe hopping, exposing attitude with wanton altercation.

Having rough sex with clingy, co-dependent countries

then sneaking away under cover of darkness. Until

one feisty little wench hides my clothes and calls her brother.

Failure

is not

an option.

Keep your black hood, your fingernail pliers.

Let me be baptized in the floodlight dancing off your scimitar.

Remember, I, too, am martyr.

As I enter the Kingdom I capture your anointed virgins

to vigorously deflower.

3.

Yesterday began with yes. My body, a carnival ride

from Intro to Demonology through Doctorate of Demise.

Riding high on rock music thighs,

leaving a trail of soft parts and liquid tongues

in a fury of unquenchable lust.

I chained you to a post and rode ever-tightening circles

in the cocaine dust until my leather steed became salt.

You checked the cuticle of your ring finger.

You, my dear, were not impressed.

Many times

the bell

has tolled.

In repose I now remain, twitching and twisted

in this damaged carcass, while you design your dances

and purple your lips and occasionally tangle

your ring finger into the matted gray

of my chest.

RIVERSIDE BLUES

Flaccid summer sky

drools damp dusk

across the sea

of silver sweat

like a revolver

kept warm in

a pool of

the victim's blood.

The flavor of

dirty fingernails in

the liquid mouth

of paid-for pleasure

on vinyl car

seats rinsed in

the storm sewer

of city evening.

MARTY THE MISOGYNIST MEETS STARDANCER

for Connie

1. Distraction

Looking a little hollow in the morning sun.

I know you'll be a screamer when the night time comes.

Struttin' bad and bold through the neon atmosphere.

No one here knows you - everyone knows you're here.

2. Connection

I transform into a false-hearted leather snake and slither up your arm.
My ivory fangs reflect in your hypnotic eyes. Fixated, swaying to the
jungle drum, the moment comes. Tight leather coils bind you. Dual
gleaming fangs thrust into your wanting throat. Your blood flames
from the poison. You would pull me loose, would you? Your fists
pound now on steel. Transfixed. Motionlessly frantic. I release to
lick the poisoned sweat from your earlobe and slither down to taste
your trembling darkness. You do not believe the false-hearted snake
but lust for my kisses.

3. Contortion

From the darkest waters rise

a scent that I have glorified.

Two streams into the rapids run

and wrestle on the rocks for fun.

Their lusty frolic finally through

they breathe out life in languid pools.

ROAD TRIP

What it is, is a three hundred fifty horsepower, Detroit steel, adrenaline injector

straddling the broken white laser line, splitting the night in two.

Your head in my lap, your feet out the window,

painted toes tickled by the dry desert wind,

you hold my tarnished Colt revolver between your legs and spin the cylinder.

What it is, is the taste of Four Roses on your tongue. Our hot breath

liquefies your candy apple lipstick, your pale eyes pierce

the deep shadows of yesterday's mascara.

We wallow like spastic canines

 in the pungent scent of ripened passion.

What it is, is neon lightning pulsing through motel room windows.

Cocooned in stiff cotton sheets, you are drifting, another life and time.

Your breath comes slow and rhythmic.

I smoke a cigarette by the window.

I hold my tarnished Colt revolver between my legs and spin the cylinder.

What it is, is circuitry, blue electric veins beneath your translucent skin.

You stand, fingertip deep, in spring water,

fingers splashing, hair plastered against sunken cheeks.

You stare into the waterfall,

nipples erect and challenging, daring to submerge.

What it is, is what it was. A nocturnal remission, somnambulistic vision.

THE BREWMASTER'S POTION

A church key of precious metal

required to enter my amber salvation.

Children of no consequence await

to facilitate my bucolic transformation,

to rejoice at my temporary disappearance.

They frolic in the transparent wasteland

setting trip wires at the edge of insolence.

They are, after all, versatile and amoebic

in their youthful flexibility.

I drift on the amber ocean

as dusk comforts me in silk sleeved arms.

No sail set, no destination, no motion,

uncharted, unencumbered channel of ceaseless drift,

horizons fading on the aromatic drink.

The foreshadowing glow seeps within,

a spider vein circulation,

warming insufficient organs through osmosis.

The anchor sinks, heavy with doubt.

Long line fishing, awaiting dark-hued dreams,

pulled from the depths to thrash about,

gills bursting red, giving up their spirit

for my emboldened fancy.

Attempts to convey their desperation

are inadequate and juvenile.

Soon they succumb, to be returned

to the depths, food for faithless cannibals.

My kin, my progeny, in connotation learned.

Exposed to darkness, innocence shocked,

stimulated, teased into recognition.

"Grow up!" I say, "You little shits!"

O faithless sun, giving up sway

with the sky. Only a cold pale shank

reflects from the lurid day

as your distant kin traipse the bounds of heaven,

the icy edges of blackness.

Pulse thunders as Maeve's terpsichorean gambol

ignites my loins. Cogency dusts away on scented winds.

Balance is freely relinquished. A gift to her frisk

and favor. O to touch. I tremble. I fall.

Plunging, limbs twisted tentacles

beneath the amber ocean,

arriving in a diseased reality amongst jovial derision.

Rust colored bottles, drained of the elixir, fly

below the sound of breaking glass and apologies.

Amnesty is unavailable to such as I.

DESERT LUST

A dusty trace where raptors rise

your steel-jacketed vision

pulling fire from cast-iron consort.

Deliquesce my flesh, my resolve

as you claw through memory

talons teasing, twisting

breaking tendons and tendrils-

your taste on my tongue-

bile of slathered rejection.

Cannibal girl with teeth of bone

rip me once & again & again.

Fallen, I'm devoured unquenched.

BAD SEED

In deep cover teeth gleam, the only light,

as through vine, limb and tearing flesh,

fresh blood dripping,

scent of life escaping.

Nature's crisis counselors recoil from the reaction.

The ivory teeth, inflamed gums, saliva dripping,

one last breath.

History records the final extinction.

The Earth exhales a putrid breath and begins to heal the wound.

Flames are created now, only by accident.

The hairless bipeds exterminate themselves through mutated greed.

The habitat sighs relief.

BLACKSMITH

Your tortured forge burns crimson,

sun's lava seen through dusty wind,

daughter's blood-stained cotton sheets.

Bellow's blast rage against the fuel.

Your hammer falls and falls again.

Your flame rises and burns within,

sweat, like wax; beading, rolling,

impassioned waves, creation's sledge.

Your hammer falls and falls again.

Heat dissipates, quells the rage.

Her lover's blood-stained garden soil

will cool your shovel's blade.

WHITE NOISE

No longer interpret strange rhythms

of asymmetric heart strings

twitching in aboriginal beats,

origins unbeknownst to

my slave trader conniptions

or fits of inorganic chemistry.

Asymmetric heart strings

sharper than razor-wire barricades

erected in haphazard patterns

against the onslaught of

flesh-covered battering rams

and case-hardened bone.

Sharper than razor-wire barricades,

free of amber reflections,

at the dark unholy mouth

of the dank night's aperture,

deep but not bottomless.

Enough liquid to encourage drowning.

Free of amber reflection

the froth filled container

devoid of content uncontaminated

by tongue lust invincibility or

a tentative loss of sanity

perverted by pillow top imagination.

The froth filled container

of empty promises gripped

between sunburned thighs

and spilled willingly on the thin

worn fabric of back seats careening

down farm to market roads.

Empty promises gripped in

the pre-frontal lobe of memory

from a time when music was

discernible from white noise

or the aboriginal beat of

strange asymmetric rhythms

STAINED

GLASS

JENSEN'S TEMPLE

Mayan Temple, Per II (Alfred Jensen) (1962)

Wafers of silicon are but

sand and water and sun

sacrificed to light

on the altar of electricity,

the angular face of

a microcircuit reflected in the

shards of a one-way mirror.

Waves of primary colors wash

over the darkness of antiquity

illuminating the brittle features

of modernism. A visionary

views the prismatic distortion,

primordial circles

of concentric construction.

Semiconductors limit cultural vision

to the intermingling of opposing forces,

creating history from the future.

AS SEEN ON TV (shout)

Rectangular God

spinning sensitive scenes

into palatable porridge.

Liquid crystals

multiply pixels

plastered against the wall.

1080 X 720 = higher math

Sleep stealing methedrine colors

shutting down synapses with mainline accuracy.

Flatline.

Flatscreen.

Slackjaw.

Codeine eyes unblinking stare.

Jupiter pupils annihilate irises

in the dark.

All ages welcome!

Available in three dimensions!

No I.D. required!

COLONIA

Water,

shared, conserved, scarce,

hand pumped with cast iron handle.

Oxide stains on galvanized pails

carried by pre- pubescent children,

barefoot, on spindle legs.

Electricity,

Anemic voltage

occasionally wheezes through spider-vein wires

suspended from tilting poles.

Often dormant compressor

in the village refrigerator

moans propitiously

to announce a brief reprieve.

Sewer,

Seriously?

Don't even go there.

Go out back

behind the partition.

Watch for snakes

and scorpions.

Brush away the spiders.

No architects are needed,

all buildings stacked and mortared,

blocks of concrete, adobe,

tan, gray, the color of milk.

Structures are low and flat

with right angle and tiny windows.

Society,

stripped of all pomp

strained to pure spirituality

and sweat,

celebrating survival.

Prosperity subjective,

the desert grants asylum

to generations.

INVOICE #14931

SANTA MARIAS CATHEDRAL

Hanging by a thread, not a thread really,

but a 600 pound test nylon strap.

Not that I need it; OSHA regs.

Still, it takes the edge off.

It's two and a half stories to the ground;

    old stories, stories from a century before air-conditioning,

    a time when stories were longer, hotter, panting for ventilation.

Dusty or damp, the atmosphere hungered for escape through the
spire.

The lawn lies below; the distance between life and death.

From my perfect perch the streets roll languidly

into the undulating countryside.

The citizens of the evening have awakened,

    gathering below in their isolation.

Those who profit from desire assemble at the oak entrance

    seeking their own redemption.

The purveyors of pleasant poisons,

    wrapped in *serapes* against the evening chill,

    tug at the wrought iron handle.

Young women, wizened faces providing solace

    to universal travelers,

temporary release to men who have mislaid the ability to love,

    slip into the shadows of the sanctuary.

Tithes are paid.

Accounts are settled.

Sinners, miscreants, transient souls seek her.

This is her house.

She needs nothing from me save my technical virtuosity.

I need nothing from her save the payment of my invoice.

 We are strangers.

 I find the fixation of the masses fascinating.

They pay their penance to the priest to seek her counsel.

One by one they approach her dank sanctorum.

They light the candle and place it among the offerings.

Each wick releases a thread of soot to grease

    the ancient wall of her chamber

    facilitating the liberation of a prayer.

 She pities the pleading pilgrims.

Tears trickle down her porcelain cheeks,

    moistening her sandals and dampening her humble garment.

As the dampness evaporates with the lengthening of the day,

    it couples with soot from the candle flames.

  Finally, melding with the tortured prayers,

    the concoction of salvation struggles toward heaven.

There exists a moment in time

    just before I slide the final tile in place,

    just prior to attaching the antiquated fastener,

    one request reaches God's ear.

THIS NEW LAND

A blister on her red-bandana skin, darkened

       by the smoke of diesel – the grime of yesterday

       and the dozens before, unredeemable history.

Her young body ages in declining circumspect,

       circle tightening, around the eyelids,

       also blistered – voided countenance of youth.

The first time she sees bones in the desert

       realizing a human femur – skeletal anatomy lesson

       taught by attached shoes – too big, but now hers.

A sweet blessing on the horizon – a windmill.

       Wait for the cover of starlight, and prayer.

       Not alone in spirit, *dólares del padre*, *El corazón de la madre*.

Forge forth, fall into the liquid ecstasy of trough.

       Water cradles her life through osmosis. Curtained by night,

       be quick. Follow the trail of discard, clothes, bodies, futures.

To prevail is to not go back, no home, *familia,*

       to find the way out or to fail and fall and fill the

       stomachs of the Caracara – to be a part of this new land.

TALISMAN

An ancient land,

   foreign to my footsteps,

   a primitive shaft pierces

   the lungs

   of Jaguar.

Last breath foams forth,

   pink and soft.

   Obsidian blade

   severs genitalia,

   pink and soft.

Jaguar rots, emasculated.

   Poached carcass stinks.

   Compost and

   vulture shit

   complete the cycle.

In my nightstand,

   in a teakwood` box

   (wrong wood and country),

   shriveled

   but rigid,

Jaguar's legacy

    pierced by latigo,

    accented

    by wooden beads,

    lies in wait.

I am adorned

    (an inferior being)

    slipping

    into night to

    play my drum.

BIPOLAR SKY

Aster field reflected in sky.

The pasty faced doughboy

smiles down at my sunburned face,

laughing at my lackadaisical whimsy,

plow abandoned,

fallow fields freshly turned.

Free, but beautifully exhausted,

if I'm not careful he'll watch me sleep.

Never has a silver lining appeared in my line of vision.

Darkness is dragged into the afternoon far too early for sunset.

Quiet broken by the next county clearing it's throat.

Time to run away.

What if I'm a lightning rod, like my dog, like my mother?

Lightning has stolen away chunks of my life,

a gruesome electric cleaver, whittling away sanity.

Run child;

away from trees, poles, tents.

Hide child;

no phones, no TVs.

Stay inside. Hunker.

Trees become toothpicks,

bodies, a twitching mass.

Air, clean, sweet.

Wind, breeze, a warm zephyr.

Sweet blossom scent.

The gritty oil from my hand on the handle of the plow.

Earth broken.

TRIGGER HAPPY

I lie dormant

in the folds of my Creator's imagination

waiting to explode,

be free of my exoskeleton,

learn to fly.

My time comes

encased in darkness

the tunnel of love.

Excitement, longing,

a fusillade of freedom awaits.

My existence, an instant

in the trace of time. Exuberant,

I span the arc of life, and death.

Penetration,

ingested by flesh.

No river of blood do I savor.

I consume no organ

just an immediate sensual dampness,

then cold air. My God has failed.

In His failure lies my predestination.

LIAR'S WORDS

Liar's words stink, mullet bloated and bursting

near brackish backwater on a red tide bay.

No pink skinned children search for shells

or form finite architecture from materials at hand.

Screaming gulls attack

and choke on liar's words.

Liar's words penetrate, a crusted gym sock

stuffing the gullet of the wallflower

under the darkened risers.

Only the sound of animal grunts,

the wet slap of skin on skin.

The broken petals of her pink rose

lie glistening on her thighs.

No one will believe.

They are the good boys.

Liar's words fulminate, a famous fable

shouted from the pulpit

while collection plates circulate.

Conscience obliterated by scattershot repentance

and a small donation.

They believe. They are the good boys.

They will not choke on liar's words.

MY CITY IS DYING

(for the victims of the 2014 SXSW tragedy)

Scrape

the last vestige of

Love & Lust & Beauty & Art

from within your fatted cheeks &

spit

onto the sizzling cement

fractured in spider-vein doubt.

Indolent insect, wary weed

emerge

to be taunted & trampled

lost to the beat

of trashman's shoes

duct taped & dreary

to dance the dirge of my city.

My city is dying

while bearded gurus ponder

hallowed museums

in cinderblock strip centers

hallucinating phantasmal visions

of Denver

& Seattle

& Tie-dye Utopia

And fail, again, to rise.

     My city is dying

while gleaming phalli

of glimmering steel

race ribbons of asphalt

over aquifer and escarpment.

Occupants, occupied with

rare metal gadgetry,

leaving empty home

for empty office.

My city is dying.

Four warm bodies

Love & Lust & Beauty & Art

now cold.

Give them names!

My city spit onto the street

Steven & Jamie & DeAndre & Sandy.

Blood soaks into spider-vein cement.

     My city is ghost.

MACHINE HEAD (shout)

My engine of consciousness trapped in a bone flask.

Only one true route of escape, past the medulla oblongata.

His chromium sword and black-iron scimitar

christened Freedom & Liberty as a taunt. Last chance:

a spinal cord, twisted bed sheets knotted together.

Escape is in the mind, awash in brutal Hope-storm

mauled against the calcite walls & stalactite pricks.

Awareness chooses alternate paths, submersing in

subcutaneous subversion, swimming roiling rivers

of plasma, platelets, and putrid poison.

Undercover of dark horror, riding the torrid nightmare

to the cycle's completion, consciousness awakens.

Another day begins.

ACTS OF GOD

(GOSPEL SONG)

Am I the one you think you seek to find?

Or did you strain against the pain

so long it made you blind?

You say, "Today you'll pay the damage of your vice."

But you know you chose to slow

and I raised the price.

I'm just a little ways away.

Not standing in the shadows anymore.

You curse the verse

that keeps repeating in your head

Some gory story

of a Hero long since dead.

You cheat your sheets of sleep

deep in the night

for if you deem to dream

 you may just die of fright.

I'm just a little ways away

Not standing in the shadows anymore.

Never a safe place to play

in the middle of the road.

If you go for a swim

better figure in the undertow.

Stacks and stacks of contracts,

notes and warranties.

Every vague disclaimer

still applies to me.

I'm just a little ways away

I'm in the shadows evermore.

BROKEN

MIRRORS

SOME DAYS

Some days are words flowing onto paper.

Some days are letters hacked into rotted wood with a dull *machete*.

Some days are words sliding from the paper and dripping like wax onto the stained concrete.

Some days the pen lies dormant, the blade of the *machete* buried in the oak headboard-

    nothing happens.

Some days are words buzzing like angry wasps, scaring children and making old men bitter.

Some days are fat bright letters, primary colors, painted on funhouse mirrors.

Some days are words tinkling softly, ice cubes in an otherwise empty highball glass,

    your green eyes reflect their sparkle as breath halts just behind my face.

Some days are letters, ghostly pale, hovering over sheets of black paper

    not quite making contact.

Some days there are no words.

WHICH POCKET?

The zippered one

or Velcro?

Where is such a thing

to be stored?

away from the sun?

close to body-

to live vicariously-

through osmosis?

Misplaced for now, again

it breathes, sighs really.

If I could follow the sound,

to redeem the broad, loud stoke

hidden somewhere,

but which pocket?

Where does it lie,

this abandoned youth?

I DON'T BELIEVE IN POETRY

I don't believe in poetry,

or God,

or space travel,

or crying on a rainy night

for no reason.

Yet

Here I am.

I believe in storytelling,

and family,

and growing old,

and energy,

and therapeutic dogs.

Yet

Here I am.

BEFORE 7 A.M.

One hen attempts to crow

perched on the wagon's tongue

relinquishing herself, a surrogate

for vacant masculinity.

Spent hens, my climbers,

follow me for melon rinds and snow peas.

In pretense, I capture them, a daily game.

Everything, everyone here escapes

but no one wanders far.

Drool faced dogs flip flop

on the cooled coals of charred earth.

Porch dogs in the afternoon,

now they frolic, wrestle and posture.

They run the lane and pastures

then wander home.

An ancient feline languishes

on the windowsill

sparring with the moss rose.

He pauses to watch me place his dish

then performs the stretch

that sends me back to bed.

CONTRAPUNTAL KISS

I. Assignment

Proprietary indifference provides entry.

Your fascination, alluring, distracting,

preposterous madness with prevailing lust.

Bloodstained image of desire, begging

to touch, to hold, to feel inside.

Returned empty and unreal, crusty and

dry, like farmer's hands.

What to do with this? You skitter away

and I am left holding nothing.

II. Pawn Shop

Proprietary indifference allows permeation.

In shadow envelope, I wait, kneeling

behind broken tools and transistors

until lights cease the florescent hum.

The lock resonates in silence so deep

Rilke's message vibrates the air.

Hearts and gizzards, souls and other plastic parts

locked in mahogany trimmed glass cases

dormant and distorted by belt buckle scratches

and children's fingerprints.

III. Opium Opus

Proprietary indifference encourages swallowing.

Years of accumulated grit grinds into my knees.

I can get up now. Can I get up now?

Dank atmosphere, thick enough to see,

wobbles around me. Beautiful porridge

spills from my cranium and splatters

on the rat-shit concrete. Head implodes.

Searching in darkness for my stolen muse,

I trigger the alarm. Imminent arrest, or escape,

or do I just break the glass?

IV. Titanium

Proprietary indifference allows escape.

Sealed and healed, feeling real,

with superhuman sass, I kick the superhero's ass.

Breaking bones. Breaking laws. Breaking free.

Mean, and oh so unclean, a sheen of sweat,

sweet smelling and slick.

Romping and stomping until the

globe shudders. Eyes burn through the

steel cartilage of skyscrapers, then

fall on you...   I am done.

SPLITTING WOOD

I'm not supposed to do this.

The muscles tighten

    around the restructured spine.

Hand eye coordination reclaimed.

Sinewy arms regain control.

The maul finds the mark.

The muscles tighten.

"Let the tool do the work."

    my father's ghost, admonishing.

Gravity on iron

Sharpened edge

seeking rift inside the grain.

"Let the tool do the work."

Guided by muscles, atrophied

    a laggard recovery. Titanium,

modern pharmacology, a year lost

to opium visitations,

mattresses, somnambulism.

Guided by muscles,

Crisp air fills lungs, replacing

    the rancid humidity of sickness.

Sunlight excites pale skin

as maul's edge penetrates oak.

Alive, again. Vital, again.

I am supposed to do this.

FORCE = GRAVITY

The gravy boat sailed

right behind the salad

across the kitchen.

    Not my fault, she said

    Accident, she said

    It just slipped

out of my hand,

out of my mouth.

Usually so calm, serene

it popped too loud

inside her head

    through her hands

    tossing the salad

    the gravy - gravity

shattered the bowl

not her fault - an accident.

One too many meals

prepared for thankless

children - husbands

   one too many

   words slurred

   one too many

late arrivals, falling

just flying, and falling.

FRACK YOU, MAMA!

Tainted snakes slithering miles below the

bedrock, spitting neurotoxins into Mother's

holy veins. She shudders; cold, sick, infected.

Her porn-poisoned parasites slide

in gleaming shells across her parched

but plasticized skin, consuming and cavorting,

oblivious to her final haggard breaths.

Cringing, as unhealed pox drain into

her nodes, exploding infectious abscesses.

Satan's surgeons steal organs,

pound with unnecessary vigor against

her remaining vitreous humor until

blindness and infirmity weaken her context.

She is shaved for further surgery.

Slowly stolen for the pornographer's

satiation of her relentless violent lover

until she's discarded, a used tire in

a whirling cooling graveyard.

In her final injustice, the pornographers,

in their ghastly flamboyance, ride her

down with no possibility of redemption.

RAPTORS

Slow motion whirlwind

still summer air stirred

by dark wings drifting,

acute eyes searching.

Redtail and Caracara

scan for life.

Vultures inhale

the scent of death.

Dancing in updrafts,

dining in prairies

with their kin.

Spending summers floating

breeze teased

feathers flutter.

Dramatic dives

disrupt the languid carousel,

quick kill,

food for further floatation.

The top of the food chain.

in a cumulus waltz.

IN MEMORIUM

"Another God-forsaken fool

 without so much as a clue."

the bellow launches the epithet into the ether.

You mean me, of course.

Standing by the stock tank

the reek of disappointment sears my nostrils.

 I have no passion for the butchering;

the boiling feathers stench my forearms

as dogs tug-o-war with gastric membranes.

Little sister giggles

at the silly death dance of fresh kill.

"Don't get any on you"

as you drain another longneck.

Now you lie in those white sheets

an overlooked dirty spatula

in a freshly bleached sink..

Another stench rises. I walk

toward the call button, never

to reach out. The mottled pate

graying, empty eyes see far, far,

far beyond me, through or around.

I am the ghost, as always.

Through your final gurgles I could not

discern, was there ever a clue?

SHARDS

ONLY WORDS

I can't find

the blue of mourning.

The spoon no longer calls

when the sun sequesters

above the roiling ceiling

of darkness,

and I wonder how

your lips do this

with only words.

SOME RANDOM TUESDAY

I took you to the River this morning to set you free

when I got home, my house wouldn't let me in.

Your sister cousin didn't miss you much,

God I love the South.

> I need nine pills

> to make it to my refill

> I can eat the rest for fun.

Sweet Jesus let the light shine in

the length of darkness seeps around me.

 Too many black cats in the gunnysack

but they pissed on the carpet, what can I say?

> St. Vitus

> grabs my face,

> shakes my body.

Judy, Judy, Judy, I never visited your grave.

We only kissed once

delivering Sunday papers

 long before daylight.

COMMUNIQUÉ 2:28 AM

My ex-lovers

    who are witches

        send me visions

            in my dreams

                to let me know

                    they are well

                        and I should stay

                            with their Sister

                              and quietly listen

                                to the Music

                                    of the Spheres

ROMANCE NOVEL

She

craved the silent majesty of the falcon

soaring over the beauty of desert vistas

picking meals from sparse mammalian ghosts.

Ocotillo and prickly-pear dared her.

A palette of daggers

painting the sunset in blood.

He

nestled his soul in the dark beauty of thicket

where eyes adjust to minimalist shadows.

Dancing around Cypress knees, his secret

lair of penitent beauty,

reptilian dangers lurking under decomposition

and tea-stained pond.

They

built a life in concrete clay compromise

where the only beauty is mathematical

symmetry of tilled fields and the dangers

are scientific and biological and posted

at the perimeter.

They loved hard.

They loved soft

and paradise cocooned around them.

INSPIRATION

You do not know me.

Yet, I am welcome

to sip your wine.

I observe your victory dance,

the ecstasy and elation

and tales of success.

I sneak into your bedroom

at the hours

between midnight and three.

Your vivid dreams

project on the beige wall

above your headboard.

I steal your diamonds,

grind them to dust

to polish my stones.

EDITOR

Slinking through horizontal strands

 of ennui and emotion,

weapon of choice,

the infamous blue pencil.

Cut and castigate,

circumcise and castrate,

The Work, prostrate,

pulp-free and bleeding

on the altar

of the creator.

KEEPER (shout)

The flipside of

 the inside of

the far side of

nowhere

 (or now here).

Your backside

silhouettes in

the bright side of

this sack of sky.

I am stuck,

mudstuck in funk

blue paralysis.

I know the words

that will spin

your body frontside

down. But loss

like dark cloth

blots the spark.

Maybe next time, Baby.

ACKNOWLEDGEMENTS

WORD GRAVY

In my youth, I went hiking in the Forest of the Muse where I came upon a roiling river of red-eye gravy. Having no spoon or dish, I cupped my hands and filled my belly. The viscous fluid was lumpy and full of words. Among the words was an occasional magician or mentalist but most were construction workers, train conductors, school teachers and clerks. I digested these words and felt satiated, content.

These words soon felt restless and began to plan their escape. Rowdy young words burst from my fingertips, celebrating on the empty white sheet, but the bonfire they danced around became their demise. Soldiers, mercenaries and several assassins tried to escape under cover of darkness, slipping under the razor wire. The more aggressive words annihilated the less persistent and continued through the fog of night.

Over the course of days, a large number of words organized into unions and became sentences and paragraphs. They staged sit-ins and protests until I was forced by my muddled conscience to release them into the media. They never looked back. No thanks did I receive.

Altruistic adjectives attempted to assist world weary nouns with a makeover before asking sweetly to be released from servitude. Seductive adverbs caressed my psyche. They teased me into submission before slipping free, leaving only their scent on my pillow. I hung their portraits in my gallery.

Words departed but words reproduced. New hybrids, formed by genetic manipulation and in-vitro fertilization, changed the Thesaurus. The Dictionary took note. An endless supply of expressions and abbreviations propelled the language toward starvation through overpopulation. There was nothing I could do. The gravy became watery and tasteless as the river left its banks, devastating the community.

I remember that glorious taste, the first sip in the Forest of the Muse. I remember the recipe for red-eye gravy.

-Tony Burnett

Marty the Misogynist Meets Stardancer first appeared in *Axis Aligned* (Summer 1985).

Road Trip won the 2012 Bruised Peach Press Poetry Award and was reprinted in the 2013 Poetry @ Round Top Festival anthology.

Blacksmith first appeared in *DNA of a Poet* anthology (TL publishing 2012).

Liar's Words and *Communiqué 2:28am* first appeared in *Vein (2013 & 2012 respectively)*.

An early version of *Acts of God* was recorded as a demo track by *The Perpetrators* for *First Offense* (1996).

Splitting Wood appeared in Toucan Literary Magazine (December 2012)

Before 7 A.M. appeared in the 2014 Texas Poetry Calendar.

First Season appeared in the 2014 Poetry @ Round Top Festival anthology

Editor has been rejected over a dozen times.

This New Land appeared in *Di-verse-city* (2016)

Cover Photography: Robin E. Burnett

Thank You

I owe a debt of Gratitude to my many mentors including Scott Wiggerman, Laurie Ann Guerrero, Charlotte Gullick, John Pipkin, Carol Dawson, Michael Noll, Nan Cuba, Joani Reese and countless others who have advised me on my journey. Also to Becka Oliver, Jennifer Ziegler, Noelle O'Donnell, Beth Sample, Jordan Smith and the supportive members of the Writers' League of Texas without whom this would have been impossible. Further thanks to Preston Burnett for helping brainstorm the artwork and to Danielle H. Acee for bringing it to fruition. Of course, my undying devotion to my trophy wife of 20+ years, Robin Burnett, not only for the outstanding cover photography but for the <u>many</u> ways she supported this project and the "long, strange trip" that lurks between these pages.

Of course, my deepest sincere appreciation to those brave folks who took the proverbial leap and bought this book by a relatively unknown poet. Thank you for taking a chance on my work. If it moved you in some way feel free to share it.

- Tony

www.ingramcontent.com/pod-product-compliance
Lightning Source LLC
Chambersburg PA
CBHW071417040426
42445CB00012BA/1190